How to Raise Healthy and Happy Children

How to Raise Healthy and Happy Children

A Pediatrician's Pearls for Parents

William Wadlington, M.D.
With
Clifton K. Meador, M.D.
And
Marietta Howington, M.A.

Authors Choice Press
San Jose New York Lincoln Shanghai

How to Raise Healthy and Happy Children
A Pediatrician's Pearls for Parents

Authors Choice Press
an imprint of iUniverse.com, Inc.

For information address:
iUniverse.com, Inc.
5220 S 16th, Ste. 200
Lincoln, NE 68512
www.iuniverse.com

ISBN: 0-595-18109-0

Printed in the United States of America

Foreword

William Wadlington, known to his friends as Bill, has practiced pediatrics for 45 years. He has seen almost all the illnesses that can occur in children. I am nearly as sure that he has seen just about every kind of strange and dysfunctional behavior that can occur in children and in parents. He has reduced much of his vast clinical experience into the tips and bits of advice contained in this book. His "pearls", as he likes to call them, are condensed statements of his wisdom.

As you will see, Bill does not make clear separations of parent from child. Clearly the child is the product of the parents. Hence you will find many pearls directed at the health and behavior of the parent. Healthy parents generate healthy children and perhaps vice versa.

Bill has been honored repeatedly by his students, his peers, and by his fellow faculty members at Vanderbilt. The teaching conference room in the Department of Pediatrics at Vanderbilt University bears his name.

In 1988, Bill Wadlington was selected as Tennessee Pediatrician of the Year. The American Academy of Pediatrics has honored him twice. In 1988, he received the National Practitioner Research Award in San Francisco for his 36 published papers. In 1991, the academy awarded him the Lay Education Award at its annual meeting in New Orleans. This award recognized his efforts in establishing the Health Hall at the Cumberland Children's Museum in Nashville. This permanent exhibit is directed at teaching children about the human body and about staying healthy.

It has been my privilege to work with Bill Wadlington in putting together this book. The pearls come from his practice experience and from his longtime friend, Marietta Howington. The pearls are aimed at helping parents raise healthy and happy children.

Clifton K. Meador, M.D.
Clinical Professor of Medicine
Vanderbilt School of Medicine
Nashville, Tennessee

Preface

In 1998, I wrote *Pearls for a Pediatric Practice I* with Clifton Meador. That book was written mainly for pediatric residents and doctors starting into practice. The book was well-received and got excellent reviews from the *Journal of the American Medical Association* (JAMA May 26, 1999. Vol. 281, No. 20)

Later that year many patients and friends said, "We want a book that offers suggestions about ways to raise our children, about discipline, etc." That is what I have attempted to do, again with the help of Dr. Clifton Meador. As I read over the material for this book, it became obvious that we did not have enough spiritual emphasis. For this important job I called on Mrs. Marietta Howington and she joined me in this effort. She also comprised the book's index.

Mrs. Howington has written for forty-two years for *Lifeway*, formerly known as the Sunday School Board of the Southern Baptist Convention. My wife and I first met Mrs. Howington twenty-seven years ago when our son, John, (and later, Jeff) were assigned to her fourth-grade class at Oak Hill Elementary School in Nashville, Tennessee. After a few weeks of her instruction, we decided she was a *master teacher.*

Mrs. Howington retired from Oak Hill in 1983, studied Braille, and then taught for nine years at the School for the Blind in Donelson, Tennessee. She has three married sons and three grandchildren. I hope this introduction will help you know Mrs. Howington better as you read some of her excellent material.

My royalties from this book will go to the Nashville Academy of Medicine Alliance (NAMA) to support the Health Hall at the Cumberland Museum and the programs of the Christie Society of Vanderbilt Children's Hospital.

William Wadlington, MD
Clinical Professor of Pediatrics
Vanderbilt Children's Hospital
Nashville, Tennessee

Acknowledgments

Dr. Clifton Meador has kept his steady hand on my writing and has put a title to each of my sayings. This random style of writing was a classic feature of his first book, *A Little Book of Doctors' Rules,* which was a remarkable success.

Clifton has written many books and articles in his varied medical career. He was Dean of the School of Medicine at the University of Alabama in Birmingham (UAB) from 1968 to 1973, when he returned to the faculty of Vanderbilt School of Internal Medicine. From 1973 to 1998, he directed the Vanderbilt residency programs in medicine and served as chief medical officer at Saint Thomas Hospital in Nashville. For the past two years he has served as Executive Director of the Meharry Vanderbilt Alliance. I am honored to have Clifton's help in preparing this book. He is the ultimate editor.

Introduction

We have enjoyed working on this book. We have a firm belief that, as a general rule, children who fit the following descriptions have better all-around health than do other children:

1. Relate rightly to family members and peers.
2. Have an inner security that comes from assimilation of spiritual values.
3. Have a daily balance between work, play, and positive family interactions.
4. Respect family members and are respected by them.
5. Have parents whose method of discipline gives children a feeling of security and leads them ultimately to self-discipline.
6. Refrain from use of tobacco, intoxicating drinks, and other addictive substances.
7. Have the security of a stable family life.
8. Live with parents whose support and guidance foster in the children an optimistic spirit that discourages tendencies toward depression and a sense of hopelessness.

Because of these convictions, we believe that pediatricians must be concerned about every facet of children's lives in order to help guide them to optimal health and wholeness.

Note:
As you read this book you will note that there is lots of information for parents (male or female). Since parents set the example for eating, exercise, good relations, etc., a pediatrician cannot help but include advice to parents in all aspects of their lives.

1. Work Can Be Wonderful

Let your children know that accomplishments don't just happen. They take work! Express the excitement of tackling life's problems and solving them.

2. Dream and Do It

"The poor man is not he who is without a cent, but he who is without a dream." Harry Kemp. If you dream you can do something, begin it. This is good advice for both parents and children.

3. None of Us Is Perfect

When parents accept the fact that they cannot be perfect, they have taken the first step to rid themselves of a guilt complex. Self-rejection can limit one's growth in parenting.

4. Some Suggestions on Ways to Choose a Physician

1. Check out credentials with the local medical association.
2. Ask neighbors what doctor they go to and why.
3. Get recommendations from a medical insider (nurses, people who work at hospitals, etc.).
4. Many physicians will agree to a brief "get acquainted" session with you. Ask if there is a charge for the visit.

5. Twin Births in the USA Are Up More than 40 Percent

The number rose from 68,339 in 1980 to 97,064 in 1994.

Reason #1: Women are having babies at older ages, and the likelihood of having twins increases with age.

Reason #2: Use of fertility drugs has increased.

6. Cultivate a Taste for Buttermilk

It has no butter and usually has very little fat.

7. Let Children Play

Most children are overwhelmed by extremely busy schedules. Children always on the run need some time to play and relax. Include this in their weekly schedules.

8. Communicate—Don't Preach

When it comes to kids and drugs, the most effective deterrent is you! The average age for first-time marijuana use is 14 years of age. Teens who've learned about drugs from their parents are one-third less likely to try pot than teens who've learned nothing. Studies show that families who eat together six to seven times a week have kids who are less apt to use drugs or alcohol.

Some Examples of Household Rules

Friends are welcome only when an adult is present.

Call home if running late.

Do homework before watching TV or socializing.

Be home by the designated curfew.

Tolerate no drug use.

10. Thought for the Day

We may give without loving, but we cannot love without giving.

11. Use What You Have

Teach children to use the talents they have, and they will not feel so strongly the need for more talents.

12. Television Is Harmful

The damage TV does to children cannot be overestimated. Some parents severely limit its use. One family turns off the tube except for once a week, the time being determined by the type of program available. They then enjoy the program together.

13. If You Fish, Teach Your Child to Fish

A teenager wrote the New York Times editor, giving his home address. He asked the editor to suggest a good place to fish not over four or five miles from his home. Said he, "My father fishes every week, but his buddies don't want boys along. I've saved enough for a rod and I could bike to the place."

The editor located the father's name in a directory and sent him the letter. "You hit me hard," said the father, "but I wish it had been sooner. I'm trying to make up for lost time."

14. Love and Discipline

Love without discipline is shallow and discipline without love is brutality.

15. Every Child Is Different

A mother boasted that she treated all children alike. What a mistake! Children have different needs. Parents should consistently love and consistently discipline, but not always in the same way for different children.

16. Distressed Parents and Distressed Children

Negative emotions have damaging effects on children. Distressed parents tend to have children who are distressed.

17. Parents Need Friends

Parents need to cultivate loyal friends. They can be great support during stressful times.

18. After Divorce

Take a long-term view toward your child's adjustment and your own after divorce. It takes children about a year to adjust to their new life, while parents often need two to three years before they feel less tense with each other and more secure with their own new lives. Helpful advice on parenting, relationships, and legal and financial matters is provided in the quarterly magazine listed below. These suggestions were not taught in medical school, but they affect about half of all our families.

Divorce Magazine, 145 Front Street East, Suite 301, Toronto, Ontario, Canada M5A 1E3 (416-368-8853).

19. Golden Rule for Parents

Praise and reward your children's good behavior!

20. Help Them Become Active and Involved

When people aren't really doing anything after school, that's where trouble starts. Children get bored and start joining the wrong crowd.

21. New Studies about an Infant's "Taste"

Contrary to popular beliefs, there is no scientific evidence that variations in early exposure to sweets permanently alters a person's preference for sweet-tasting foods. The preference for salt that emerges at 4 months appears to be largely unlearned.

22. Steam Instead of Boiling

Vegetables generally lose 50 percent less minerals during steaming than with boiling.

23. Try Pink

Ounce for ounce, pink grapefruits and white grapefruits are about the same in calories, but the pink variety has forty times the beta-carotene.

24. Tips for Parents on Managing Tantrums

1. Minimize the need to say "No" by storing breakable items.

2. Use distraction. When frustration begins to mount, redirect the child to a more acceptable activity.

3. Present choices within the limits of what is acceptable. For example, "Do you want to wear your red pajamas or your blue ones?"

4. Pick your battles carefully. The more important the issue (for example, safety precautions), the more likely you are to be firm and consistent.

5. When a preschool child throws a tantrum, stay within the child's sight, carrying on normal activities without talking to him.

6. For the older child, establish the rule that he must go to his room until he calms down. When a tantrum occurs, tell him to leave, but do not lecture, threaten, or argue.

7. Use words such as "out of control" instead of "bad child" to describe tantrum-throwing behavior, and praise the child's ability to regain control after a tantrum.

8. Once a tantrum is over, the child is entitled to start over with a clean slate. Comfort may be given, but any original demands the child had should not be fulfilled.

9. Try to establish an environment of positive reinforcement in the household by commenting on and praising desirable or neutral behavior.

25. Talk with Children

Parents need to talk with their children rather than to, for, or at them.

26. Some Ways to Build Self-esteem in a Child

1. Emphasize exploring over explaining.
2. Avoid directing your child by saying, "Do this," or "I said." Try, "How about?"
3. Don't set a limit you can't enforce.
4. Hold high expectations but don't let the expectation form the ultimate judgment if the child doesn't quite meet the expectation. Instead, celebrate the positive.
5. Try not to connect learning with school, since learning "occurs anywhere in life where you have a goal and a personal challenge."

27. Don't Assume that a Wine Cooler Is "Light"

It isn't! A 12-ounce bottle has more alcohol than 12 ounces of beer, 5 ounces of wine, or 1 ounce of liquor.

28. Watch Your Calories

To remove fat from a soup, stew, gravy or sauce, refrigerate it—the fat will rise to the top and congeal, making for easy removal.

29. Water a Cat

If a cat behaves unacceptably—for example, biting a young child or clawing the furniture—say "No!" in a loud, sharp voice and then spray the cat with water from a plant mister. After four to six weeks, just the "No!" will suffice.

30. Housework

Housework is something you do that nobody notices unless you don't do it.

31. Ends of Ropes

This old advice is still good: "When you get to the end of your rope, tie a knot and hang on."

32. Know the Parents of Your Children's Friends

Delay your child's visit to another child's home until you come to know the parents and their lifestyles. Tactfully ask school and church leaders about the other child. And check with the parents about your own child's behavior!

33. Learn to Say "No"

"The ability to say 'No' is perhaps the greatest gift a parent has." Sam Levenson

34. Sowing and Reaping

"Sow an act and you reap a habit. Sow a habit and you reap a character. Sow a character and you reap a destiny."

35. Optimism

Children need optimistic persons as role models. To the pessimist, opportunities become difficulties. To the optimist, difficulties become opportunities.

36. Seek Help

Years ago, parents and teachers almost never heard of students taking drugs or getting pregnant. Not so anymore. Parents dealing with these problems should know it's never too late to seek help. Begin with the school counselor.

37. Don't Neglect Your Lips When Applying Sunscreen

The lower lip is one of the most common sites for skin cancer.

38. The Ears Have It

This year physicians will record an estimated 30 million office visits for middle ear infections. An estimated 40 percent of pediatric practice during the first three years of life is devoted to this condition.

39. The Compound That Makes Tomatoes Red
Lycopene may not only help prevent prostate cancer. It may also treat it.

40. Another Use for Old Newspapers
Drying your exercise shoes with a heater or clothes dryer can damage the shock-absorbing midsoles. Stuff them with newspaper, which will help them dry.

41. Don't Choke Your Child
Remove drawstrings from hoods and necks of children's clothing, or at least cut the strings as short as needed to close the garment. Drawstrings can get caught on playground equipment, an escalator, a fence, or elsewhere. Also tie knots in the cords of your venetian blinds. Children can "hang themselves" on the cords!

42. Reduce Your Chances of a Car Accident
Use of auto lights during the daylight hours is standard procedure in Canada and has reduced accidents there by more than 10 percent.

43. Sunburns Should Be Out
Emphasize to your children that "tan is no longer cool or beautiful." It can lead to wrinkles and premature aging of the skin. Remind teens that persons "in the know" use sunscreen moisturizers and cover-up creams to help them look more attractive.

44. Homework Comes First—Without TV
Children who have television sets in their rooms tend to watch more television with less supervision. Suggest keeping TV sets in a family room where parents can "tune in" regularly. One inflexible rule should be that homework must be done apart from TV viewing.

45. Always Eat the Skin

Ounce for ounce, the skin of the potato has far more fiber, potassium, and B vitamins than the flesh.

46. Responsibilities of Parents

A parent told her child's teacher, "I'm not responsible for everything my son does." "Right," said the teacher. "But you are responsible for seeking guidance from teachers, school counselors, pastors, books, or other sources. And don't forget daily prayer."

47. I Have Today

I have no yesterdays; time took them away; tomorrow may not be—but I have today.

48. A Parent's Prayer

You will do this prayer no harm if you include the italicized words: "Let the words of my mouth, and the meditation of my heart, *and the deeds of my life*, be acceptable in thy sight, O Lord, my strength and my redeemer" (Psalm 19:14). God's help is available to all parents.

49. Solve Small Problems

The biggest problems in the world could have been solved when they were small.

50. If You Want to Be a Good Father

Be a good husband first.

51. When Hands Feel Almost Numb in Freezing Weather

Swing your arms in a circle like a baseball pitcher's windup. This brings blood rushing to your hands and warms them up fast.

52. Read the Right Stuff

You can greatly aid your child by the right selection of reading matter for your home. George Trevelyan said, "Education has produced a vast population able to read but unable to distinguish what is worth reading."

53. Make Leaning Unnecessary

"A mother is not a person to lean on but a person to make leaning unnecessary." Dorothy Canfield Fisher

54. Convey Your Acceptance

Children feel accepted only when parents find ways to convey that acceptance. Starters: "Tell me about it." "What's your opinion?" "What can we do about it?"

You must accept your child just as she is before you can mold her significantly into what she needs to become.

55. Brighten Up Early

As soon as possible after you awaken, expose yourself to bright light—preferably sunlight. This will help you become alert faster.

56. Exercise Is Great!

Frequent, intermittent exercise helps keep your mind and body sharp as you grow older.

57. Humor Helps Keep You Healthy

Take a humor break every day to read jokes and laugh. A sense of humor improves your sense of well being.

58. Shy Children

A woman made this observation about her childhood: Let a shy child develop into a social being in her own good time. I was never told I was shy. No one said such things as "Answer the lady! Has the cat got your tongue?" Thus, I never felt inferior and overcame extreme shyness in time.

59. Fire Safety

Never let your child wear cotton or cotton-blend sleepwear; it is highly flammable and ignites easily.

60. Mothballs Toxic If Ingested

Mothballs are toxic when ingested. Remove mothballs from all closets, drawers, and other places where children are apt to go.

61. What Is the Response of 8- to 10-Year-Olds to Divorce?

This age group usually responds with anger. In general, boys tend to externalize their anger over divorce, fighting with classmates and lashing out at the world. Girls, however, tend to internalize their feelings, becoming anxious, withdrawn, and depressed.

62. Another Cause for a Weakened Immune System

An Ohio State University study found that a network of close friends helps prevent stress-related declines in the immune system.

63. Doctors Need to Give More Advice

Physicians asked 70% of their office patients ages 11-21 whether they smoked. However, physicians provided information and advice about cessation of smoking for only 2% or these patients.

64. They Don't Look Like the Rest of the Family

In mental retardation, reduced family resemblance is one of the best indicators that the cause is an abnormal chromosome.

65. As Guests in Other People's Homes

1. Do not allow your children to go to others' homes until they can behave appropriately.

2. Make a list of manners that should be followed at your home as well at others' homes.

3. Review this list daily (not hitting others, saying "please" and "thank you," talking quietly, sharing, etc.).

4. Daily set these examples yourself in your home.

5. Let them know that appropriate behavior determines whether they can visit again soon.

66. Spanking and Punishment

Don't administer any punishments while in a state of anger. Spanking children to correct or control their behavior may seem to work in the short term, but may have the opposite effect in the long term.

Parents are more likely to use harsh techniques of discipline when they are angry, irritable, depressed, fatigued, or stressed.

In one study, about ¾ of parents expressed anger, remorse, and agitation while punishing their children. Most parents cannot "spank" their children in a calm, planned way.

67. Advice from the American Academy of Pediatrics

Parents who spank are more likely to use other forms of corporal punishment and a greater variety of verbal and other punitive methods. When punishment fails, parents who rely on it tend to increase the intensity of its use rather than change strategies.

An excellent source of discussion and reference on this subject: "The Short and Long Term Consequences of Corporeal Punishment" in *Pediatrics* (October, 1996, Vol. 98, No. 4, Part 2 of 2)

68. Make Food Taste Good without Too Much Salt
To cut down on salt intake, try adding a few drops of lemon juice to foods.

69. Think Before You Speak
If you have to make a speech, remember: It's five times harder to command the ear than to catch the eye!

70. Now Hear This
If you have a "quiet baby," one who doesn't babble in the first few months, who doesn't turn her eyes to you when you are speaking: get her hearing checked quickly. Do not wait until there is marked speech delay.

For more information on speech, language, or hearing problems, contact the American Speech-Language-Hearing Association at (800) 638-825 or the Stuttering Foundation of America at (800) 992-9392.

About 5 percent of children (grades one through twelve) have some sort of speech disorder.

71. What's Happening to Mom and Fetus at 33 Weeks?
The fetus is exercising its lungs by practicing breathing—inhaling amniotic fluid. Mom is gaining a pound a week now; roughly half of that goes right to the fetus. In fact, the baby-to-be gains 50 percent of its birth weight during the next seven weeks.

72. Dust Mites Frequently Trigger Asthma Attacks
If you are allergic to dust mites and suspect that your area rugs make you sneeze and itch, place the rugs outdoors in direct sunlight. In one study,

researchers placed mite-infected rugs upside-down on an outdoor concrete surface during a summer day. After four hours, no live mites or eggs survived. Airing rugs and other household items outdoors dries and warms them, a process that kills mites.

73. You May Want to Know Quickly!

Urine pregnancy tests will demonstrate positive results 7 to 10 days after conception, before the next menstrual period is missed.

74. Grandmother Was Right Again

Chicken soup is an effective decongestant. *The New England Journal* of *Medicine* has reported that it contains substances that dilate bronchial tubes and substances that help prevent white cells from migrating to the bronchial areas.

75. Is an Allowance a Healthy Tool in Raising Children?

Automatic raises should not be assured because a child is getting older. This isn't a good picture of the real world.

Allowances should be given for various jobs around the house or yard. There is NO FREE LUNCH. The child will be proud of the accomplishments she did without outside help. A generous allowance will vary with different families, but there should also be deductions for failed accomplishments.

You are training them for the real world where financial planning plays a major role, along with self-discipline and delayed gratification.

76. What Factors Make Acne Treatment Fail?

1. A reluctant teenager who doesn't cooperate.
2. Initial treatment too strong.
3. A quick first visit with inadequate instructions and poor follow-up.

4. Failure to give patient a prescription schedule handout.

5. Strong family history of acne on both sides of the family.

6. Patient not told the prescription may irritate the skin.

77. Never Compare One Child to Another

"You should be more like your brother." "Stop mumbling! Speak up!" "Look at me when I speak to you!" Such remarks cause resentment and lower self-esteem. Get shy children into activities that call for social interaction. Above all, remember: Children who feel completely accepted as they are usually develop eventually in acceptable ways.

78. Be Kinder, Be Blinder

An elderly mother advised her daughter: "Major on behavior with major consequences. Be a little blind to behavior which a child will quickly outgrow."

This advice is reminiscent of Edgar Guest's poem:

Let me be a little kinder,
Let me be a little blinder
To the faults of those around me,
Let me praise a little more.

79. Add to Life

A mother taught her children: "We are here to add to life, not to strive for what we can get from it."

80. A Laugh a Day

The most lost day of all is the day on which we do not laugh.

81. Show Your Love

If you want with all your heart to tell someone that you love him, say as little as possible about it, and show him in loving deeds.

82. Firm Control Pays Off

A teacher related this true story about a couple in Louisville, Kentucky who had no TV until their children married. They also limited their children's visits to homes where strict controls were not set for TV viewing. Both children became outstanding, secure, happy adults and follow the same pattern for their own children.

83. Comic Books

Do you peruse every comic book before letting your children buy it? Know what they are reading!

84. Be Accessible to Your Children

Some say, "I give my children quality time." But children benefit best by the gift of quantity time. Few things are more important in child development than frequent parental accessibility.

85. On Commending Children

It's fine to commend children for good grades. It's even better to commend them for being honest, compassionate, respectful, generous, and truthful. A word of caution: You will teach only those values that you demonstrate in your own life.

86. In the Car

Establish rules for driving and riding in the car so that everyone will be calmer and safer.

87. We Keep Repeating: Parents Must Set the Example

Diets that are filled with fruits and vegetables instead of fats—along with exercise and weight control—could reduce cancer incidence eventually by 30 to 40 percent. That would amount to 3 million to 4 million fewer cases per year worldwide. Diet and lifestyle may be particularly effective in preventing America's four leading malignancies: prostate, breast, colon, and lung cancer.

88. You Don't Need a Room Full of Toys
The real key to boosting your child's development—and more important than fancy computer games, toys, or gadgets—is your love and nurturing.

89. Childhood Cancer
Most people who survive childhood cancer can rest assured that their offspring are no more likely to develop cancer than other children are.

90. Foods That Help Prevent Some Types of Cancer
1. Garlic, broccoli, cauliflower, and other cruciferous vegetables
2. Grapes and most fruits
3. Soy foods
4. Green tea

91. Warm Your Inhaler in the Wintertime
Athletes who participate in sports during the winter seasons may find that cold air is an additional trigger beyond the exercise itself. Breathing through the nose pre-warms inspired air. Or athletes may wear a scarf over their mouths to pre-warm the air.

92. It Will Save You Money
Pills are frequently cheaper than the same dose as a liquid. Also it is usually cheaper to order a double strength pill (i.e., 200mg) and cut it in half if you need to get 100 mg twice a day. A pill cutter can be purchased

at the drugstore if necessary. Check with your doctor. You may not want to cut sustained release tablets.

93. Learning Problems
Most children do not outgrow their learning disabilities, but they tend to compensate for them and adjust to them.

94. Bedtime Activities for "Sleepy Time"
1. Sing and hum lullabies and tell stories.
2. Hold the child on your lap as you tell or read a bedtime story.
3. Let her sleep with a soft toy.
4. Don't say, "Do you want to go to bed?" Say: "Now it is bedtime. I'll see you in the morning."

Toddlers who feel loved usually grow up confident and optimistic.

95. Good Schools
Kids attach meanings to sounds before they "shed their diapers," and they analyze grammar by age 3.

96. When to Get Your Child Checked
By 3 months: Does not turn his head to your speech
7–12 months: Does not imitate speech sounds from parents
1-2 years: Cannot point to book pictures that you name
2–3 years: Cannot name common objects or put 2 or 3 words together
3–4 years: Cannot be understood by main family people, or use 4-word sentences
Your doctor will especially want to know about the child's motor development and hearing.

97. Abuse Has Long-Term Effects

In adults who were abused as children the memory-making area of the brain is smaller than in nonabused adults. This effect is believed to be the result of the toxic effects of excessive cortisol.

98. Read to Your Child

About 50% of all parents say that they read to their child daily; 55 percent of parents say they sing or play music for their child daily. About 25% of parents say their child plays with a computer or computer game.

99. More on Child Abuse

Since 1980, annual reports of incidents of child abuse and neglect have risen threefold, to more than 3 million. Children under 1 year of age account for one third of reported physical abuse cases, with head trauma the most frequent cause of disability or death.

100. Always Look Up

Never look down on anyone unless you are pulling him up.

101. Serious Talk about a Serious Matter

Before your teenager is allowed to drive or be in cars with other teenagers who drive, have a serious talk and establish rules.

102. Fatherless Families

One of our worst social problems is the breakdown of the family. A chief factor is the absence of fathers.

103. Speech Is Wonderful

The dinner table is a good place to revive the grandeur of the English language. To start, teach children to replace, "I'm like, 'Gimme a chance!'" with, "I said, 'Give me a chance!'"

104. On Being Honorable

It's more important for your children to be honorable than to be on the honor roll.

105. Model Behaviors

Dr. Laura Schlessinger suggests: "Instill respect for authority in your children by modeling that behavior. Establish consequences for moral lapses and follow through. Eat meals together and explore moral issues. Attend worship services regularly as a family. Pay attention to what your children watch, read, and listen to."

106. Two Tragedies

George Bernard Shaw: "There are two tragedies in life: One is not to get your heart's desire; the other is to get it."

107. Love, Security, and School Work

Children who feel loved are more secure and do better in school.

108. Vocabulary and Talking

A University of Kansas study concluded that children of talkative parents knew more words than other children. Those who tested at the highest levels had been exposed to more than three times the amount of spoken language than the children who scored the lowest. You can greatly increase your child's intelligence by conversing with him.

109. Security in Discipline

We've heard that there is security in discipline. It sometimes must be firm. Dr. Olin Binkley had a two-year-old whom he had cautioned a couple of times to "leave Daddy's books on the shelves." The next day, she had scattered them all over the floor. He spanked her on the buttocks, which he humorously said, "God made this fatty part of the human anatomy with parents in mind." Then he picked her up and loved her. Said he, "I don't say this discipline is always right. I can say only that she never did it again."

110. Start Reading Early

Read to your young child. It can help him understand the mechanics of reading. Children who learn to read before first grade will score higher on standardized tests.

111. Parent Reform Comes First

Only about half of eighth graders' parents have any contact with their children's schools. We will never see lasting school reform until we first see parent reform.

112. Television, Homework, and Reading

Eighth graders spend an average of 21.4 hours a week watching TV but only 5.6 hours doing homework and 1.8 hours on outside reading. Nearly 65 percent report that their parents rarely or never limit the amount of TV these youngsters watch.

113. Tips for Mealtime

1. Set a good example. Children often will eat what they see you eat.
2. Don't use food as a reward.
3. Allow children to eat with other family members.
4. Invite your child to help with meal preparation. Children will eat what they help make.
5. Serve small portions on small plates. Let them ask for more.
6. Teach and reinforce good table manners.
7. Remain calm if children leave a lot on their plates. They don't have to "clean the plates."
8. Make mealtime a fun, positive experience.
9. Praise your child at the end of a good meal.

114. Make a "Chore Poster"

Divide a large poster into sections to equal the number of your children. Let each child list his chores and illustrate each chore with colorful drawings. Display drawings. Commend children who do well. Encourage those who occasionally forget.

115. Teach Your Children Who and Where They Are

Make sure your child can recite your telephone number, street address, and two of the neighbors' names, and knows what to do in an emergency.

116. Traveling with Children

A grandmother tells this story: Our grandchildren and their parents started for the Grand Canyon from Tennessee. When they got to their city's outskirts, the 5-year-old asked, "Are we nearly there?" Luckily, parents had provided games, coloring books, puzzles, storybooks, and other activities to keep the children occupied.

117. Learn to Handle the Bad Things

You are not responsible for all the "bad" things that come your way, but you *are* responsible for how you handle them!

118. Three Rules for the Child Who Stutters

1. Do not correct stuttering because that only makes the child more self-conscious.
2. Do praise fluency.
3. Allow the child time to talk, avoiding the temptation to try to hurry him along or to complete sentences or phrases for him.

119. Do You Have Someone Missing?

Three-quarters of a million children under age 18 are reported as missing every year. The National Center for Missing and Exploited Children hotline is 1-800-845-5678.

120. Why Is This So?

The incidence of suicide among teenagers and young adults has nearly tripled over the last 50 years.

121. Is It "Flu" or a "Bad Cold?"

For the diagnosis of flu, remember the two "S" words "SUDDEN" and "SEVERE."

122. Am I Special to You?

Make sure that each child feels special and loved in her own way. One certain way to instill jealousy is to tell your child how unfavorably she compares to another child, be it a sibling, a neighbor or a playmate. Saying to a brother or sister, "Why aren't you like so-and-so?" is a sure way to create intractable jealousy deep in the soul of a child. Jealousy operates on the basis of insecurity and anxiety.

123. Four Ways to Tell If Your Child Gets Enough Attention at School

1. Does the teacher really know my child? During parent-teacher meetings, can the teacher give specifics about a child's performance and behavior?

2. Does the teacher comment on assignments? Teachers who have one-on-one relationships with students offer constructive criticism, not just a letter grade.

3. Does my child talk about special things her teacher notices about her? Young children are excited when a teacher notices things like new shoes or a missing tooth.

4. Is my child excited or turned off by school? Children should believe that they are an important part of their classroom and that their teacher cares about them.

If you feel your child is not getting enough help, ask for a conference with the teacher to see how you both can "work together."

124. How Large Should Classes Be?
The average class in grades 1 through 3 has 22 students. Generally speaking, the smaller classes are the better ones.

125. Sibling Squabbles
Let your children resolve a dispute if possible, but if things get heated, don't be afraid to step in and offer ideas for solutions. You may be able to mediate a compromise, and your children can learn from your negotiating talents.

126. "Beach Week" Is a High School Graduation Rite
Talk with your teenagers and let them know what to expect during "beach week." They can expect a significant percentage of the kids to engage in serious risk-taking behavior (especially alcohol and drugs). Some will be looking for SUDS AND SEX, others for SAND AND SUN, but all should keep their SANITY. Your children should be prepared with medical insurance ID cards.

127. Learn Just to Say "NO"...Very Politely
1. "I'm flattered by your request, but...."
2. "I'm honored that you thought of me, but...."

128. Count Your Child's Breathing Rate Before Calling Your Doctor

A child's rate of breathing may be as good or better than a stethoscope in determining if a child has pneumonia. Count the number of breaths for a full minute. Always call if the rate is over 50 breaths per minute.

129. Ask Your Doctor to Talk with Your Teenagers about Smoking

Most physicians do not counsel teens about the risks of smoking, even after they identify youths as smokers.

130. All Pus in the Nose Isn't "Sinus"

If a child has a "viral cold," the virus can stimulate enzymes to draw in white blood cells (white blood cells make up what we see as pus). Therefore, many viral upper respiratory infections produce pus. This is part of the natural history of viral infections. But if this goes on for 10 to 14 days, the likelihood of sinusitis increases, and the condition should be treated with antibiotics.

131. I-Can-Do-It-Myself Software

Children are motivated to play with things that interest them. They want highly interactive programs that ensure rapid success. Look for software that provides many choices and puts the child in control.

132. Mother's Diet Affects Flavor and Amount of Breast Milk

Breastfeeding babies may develop a preference for the flavors of food their mothers consume most often. Newborns not only like sweet flavors, but sweet tastes appear to have a soothing, even analgesic, effect on them. Contrary to folk wisdom, babies drink less breast milk—not more—when their mother consumes alcohol shortly before nursing.

Babies can't detect saltiness until they are 4 months old.

133. "Mother, What Is Today's Date?"

Don't give your child a direct answer. Ask her, "What would be a way to find out?" The child might answer later, "Look in the front of the newspaper." Then say, "Good thinking." Encourage children to ask questions, and don't always answer directly. Instead, guide them in finding the answers.

134. Listen to the Answers of Your Children's Questions

Your child asks, "Daddy, where do rainbows come from?" You say, "What do you think?" Then listen to her wonderfully creative ideas.

135. Children Need Challenges

Try not to do the puzzle for your child; just be there to help if he gets frustrated.

136. Children's Fears Are Learned!

The origins of many childhood fears can be found in everyday life. By listening to your child for the clues that lead to his fears, you can help him begin to understand and manage them. Children can learn to be afraid of almost anything.

137. Overweight Adolescents

In men, risks from all causes of death and coronary heart disease are twice higher in those who had been overweight as adolescents as compared with those whose weight had been normal. About half of overweight adolescents remain overweight in adulthood.

138. Why Is My Blood Pressure Up?

The prevalence of hypertension is much greater in blacks than whites. No one knows why. Genetic factors may play a part. Systolic pressure is controlled by two sets of genes: one at rest and the other during exercise. We now attach more importance to systolic pressure than was true in previous times.

139. Another Good Fact about a Good Food
Eat a banana every day. Potassium prevents plaque buildup on artery walls.

140. Exercise—Is More Better? Is Some Enough?
No one knows the right amount of exercise for various people and age groups. We recommend the following (and it's free!).

1. Walk at least 30 minutes daily.
2. Walk briskly (3 to 4 miles per hour).
3. Three to four times per week—walk faster than usual until your breathing becomes more pronounced.
4. As you can see, SOME IS GOOD, but MORE IS BETTER.

141. Seatbelts
Make sure your children's seatbelts and your own are always fastened. Offenders should be strictly disciplined.

142. Spanking
The best study ever done on discipline trends found that parents who never spanked children were more likely to fly into physical rages than those who occasionally spanked moderately when occasion demanded.

143. On Saying "No"
A couple resolved, when their first child was born, never to say "No." Eight years later, every time they asked their son to do something, he shouted, "No!"

144. On Nurturing
No matter what else they're doing, women should be always nurturing.

145. Notes to Grandparents
Over four million American youngsters live with grandparents, many in stressful circumstances. Grandparents, contact AARP's Grandparent Information Center for help. (AARP: P.O. Box 199, Long Beach, CA 90801)

146. Strong-Willed Children
To deal with strong-willed children: Find ways to help strong-willed kids feel unique and special. Avoid phrases such as "you must," "you have to" or "no way are you going to do...." Choose battles—don't make everything non-negotiable. Lighten up but don't let up. Make sure the child knows he is loved unconditionally.

147. Being Calm Is Healthy
Anything that leads to a calming effect is almost always good healthcare. Stress is deadly. Prayer, for many people, has an anti-stress effect.

148. Children Need to Practice Politeness
Children will learn to be polite when given opportunities to practice being polite and when they are praised for their efforts.

149. The Fabric of Parenting
A person who is rightly related to God and to human beings and who keeps an optimistic outlook has woven important strands in the fabric of parenting. We can impart to our children only what we already possess.

150. On Introducing Prayer
A parent's best gift to a child may be an introduction to prayer. Begin with something like, "Now I lay me down to sleep...." Soon he will say a few words, which grow into full prayers in time.

151. Give What Money Cannot Buy

Concentrate less on giving your child things money can buy and more on things money cannot buy.

152. Children Watch What We Do

What you do or say to others speaks louder than countless reminders to your child to "be nice."

153. On Avoiding Fighting

Let children cool off after a fight. Then encourage them to think of a solution that will avoid further fights. If they succeed, give them a pat on the back.

154. Choose Your Words Carefully

Care must be taken to avoid suggesting that the deceased person "went to sleep." This explanation may create undue fears in children that they might die while asleep.

155. Dry and Wet Brushing

Brushing without toothpaste may be better at removing plaque than brushing with toothpaste. Then, after dry brushing, a thirty-second brushing with toothpaste helps remove stains and provides cavity-fighting fluoride.

156. Curb the Fat!

The more muscle you build, the more calories you burn, day or night, running or sitting. Lean muscle tissue is 17 to 25 times more active than fat.

157. You Can't Beat Exercise

For every 30 minutes you exercise, you add 60 minutes to your life!

158. Risky Business: Minors Who Are Alone at Home

Working parents let as many as 15 million latchkey children come home from school to an empty house each day, the Education Department estimates. Fully 85 percent of adults say it's hard to find after-school programs for children and teens. Latchkey kids now average 20 to 25 hours alone each week.

159. What About the Child Who Cheats?

Children don't cheat because they're bad, educators say, but because they want to be good—to please parents and teachers and succeed in school and sports.

160. How to Get the Best Possible Care from Your Doctor

1. Communicate your needs clearly.
2. Bring a list of your problems and get them all answered.
3. If you're pleased with how your doctor has helped you, let him know. You might say, "That was such a thorough examination."
4. Referrals are the sincerest expression of appreciation. Your doctor will feel deeply gratified if new patients come at your suggestion.
5. If your doctor fails to make things clear to you, tell him. Instead of blaming him, consider assuming some responsibility for the poor communication.
6. Don't say, "You are always late, and I can't stand it." Say, "When is the best time for my next appointment so that I won't have to wait so long before I can see you?"

161. Do Things Together

The best way to establish a good relationship with your child: Do things together regularly: run errands; do garden work; get a meal; play a game.

162. On Expressing Emotions

Help children express negative emotions appropriately: hammer a pegboard; crush clay; punch a bag; swim; describe feelings on paper.

163. Tape Numbers to Your Telephone

Glue a strip of paper to the bottom of your phone. List all numbers your child may need to call in an emergency.

164. Facts About Adolescent Suicide

Now, think hard about these facts:

1. Suicide represents the second leading cause of death among 15-19 year olds.
2. Since 1950, the suicide rate for adolescents has more than tripled.
3. Most suicidal adolescents do not want suicide to happen.
4. Nine out of ten adolescents who commit suicide give clues to others before the suicide attempt. Warning signs for adolescent suicide include depressed mood, substance abuse, loss of interest in once-pleasurable activities, decreased activity levels, decreased attention, easily distracted, isolation, withdrawing from others, sleep changes, appetite changes, devising morbid ideas, offering verbal cues ("I wish I were dead"), offering written cues (notes, poems), and giving possessions away.
5. A survey of 16,000 teenagers found that 20 percent had seriously considered attempting suicide in the previous year!
6. Males are 4-5 times more likely than adolescent females to complete a suicide attempt.

165. Facts About Adolescent Homicide

1. Homicide is the third leading cause of death in the 15-19 age group.
2. Guns (in 1994) accounted for 67 percent of all completed adolescent suicides.

3. Hanging, not drugs, was second.

4. Homes with guns increased an adolescent's risk by four times.

166. What Can a Parent Do About Suicide?

1. Don't keep guns in your home.

2. Listen to your child when she gives warning signs of suicide. (see above).

3. Get help and counseling.

167. American Foundation for Suicide Prevention

This foundation provides research, education, and current statistics regarding suicide. Links to other suicide and mental health sites are offered. Membership opportunity is available (see www.afsp.org).

168. Suicide and Personal Worth

In 1985, 90 percent of adolescents who attempted suicide intensely doubted their personal worth.

169. Don't Do Too Much

Doing too much for children destroys self-esteem. The more children do for themselves and for others, the more they try to meet their own needs and those of others.

170. "As He Thinketh in His Heart, So Is He" (Proverbs 23:7, KJV)

Be sure your child thinks of himself as a capable and significant person.

171. Know Your Child's Strengths and Weaknesses

Analyze your child's weaknesses and strengths. Without making your aim apparent, work slowly to strengthen her weak areas.

172. Each Child Has Infinite Worth
If we convince our children of their unique, infinite worth, we will help them become happy, well-adjusted children.

173. "God So Loved that He Gave..."
Help children discover ways to give love. Together, take outgrown toys and clothes to charity organizations. Send handmade cards to those who need them. Find other projects.

174. Swallow Evil Words
"By swallowing evil words unsaid, no one has harmed his stomach." Sir Winston Churchill

175. Joyful Hearts
The most important piece of luggage is a joyful heart.

176. Producing Fear or Anxiety in Children Is Wrong
Do not make statements like these:
"Drink your milk or your teeth will fall out." "Take your medicine or we'll have to go back to the doctor."

177. On Doing Things Well
A child needs to feel she can do some things well. This assurance makes her less fearful about trying new things.

178. What Makes a Good Friend?
"A friend is one who knows all about you and loves you just the same." Charles Kingsley

179. Is a Pacifier Thermometer Accurate?

When half a degree is added to the pacifier's reading, the results have been identical to those obtained with the rectal thermometer.

180. Praise Process

The best way to motivate kids is not with words of praise about the outcome, but with words of encouragement about the process. Choose your words carefully.

181. Smoking Is Not the Best Way

As a means of staying thin, smoking is a poor bargain.

182. Try It and Then Dump It

Seventy percent of Tennessee high school students have tried cigarettes and forty percent of middle-school students have done the same.

183. Grandparents

Keep all pills out of reach of children, including grandparents' pills when they come to visit.

184. Safe Electrical Cords

Don't run electrical cords under carpets. This can cause a fire!

185. Red Bottoms

Most diaper rashes will respond best to frequent diaper changes and "keeping the bottom dry." A hair blower works well. Ammonia in the urine is not the culprit.

A fungus, commonly called thrush, is the most common complication of irritant diaper rash.

Cleaning after urination is not necessary, only after bowel movements.

186. Take an Aspirin and Call an Ambulance

If you think you are having a heart attack, call an ambulance and chew a non-coated aspirin. Chewing before swallowing gets the clot-busting action of aspirin into your bloodstream quicker.

187. When You Fail as a Parent

Don't fret over parental failures. All parents feel they have let down their child at some time or another. Pick up the pieces and keep going. The past is in the past; leave it there.

188. Perception of Safety

Learning when and where children feel safe reveals a great deal about their risks and the steps they might take to lower risk. Ask: "Are there lots of fights at your school?" "Do people bring weapons to school?"

189. School Work: What Should Parents Do?

1. When a child begins school he should understand that homework and grades are between him and his teacher. This does not mean that parents fail to require that homework be finished before watching TV or following other pursuits.
2. The child alone should feel responsible for his successes and failures in school.
3. Parents should continuously encourage learning and thinking at home. They should listen to the child with their full attention.
4. Parents must convey that they respect both the school system and the teachers (at least in the presence of the child).
5. Nagging about school promotes rebellion.
6. Bribes for good grades are shortcuts that rarely work well.

190. Allow Your Children to Fail!

Get out of their way and let them experiment. They will learn more from their mistakes than their successes. Failure can be a great learning experience.

191. Relearn How to Play

One of the wonderful gifts children give to parents is the opportunity to relearn how to be playful.

192. A Gold Nugget for Parents

"To be what we are and to become what we are capable of becoming is the only end in life." Robert Louis Stevenson

193. Important Questions Concerning Your Child

If your child wishes to spend the night with a friend, seek answers to these questions:

1. Will they have adult supervision?
2. Will adults monitor TV and computer?
3. Is there a loaded gun in the home?

194. Be Suspicious of All Injuries Under Two Years of Age

Inflicted head trauma is the leading cause of death and morbidity from child physical abuse during infancy. Many of these young victims of violent shaking and/or inflicted cranial impact demonstrate evidence of previous cranial trauma at the time of initial diagnosis.

195. Good Stats

A recent study showed: Juvenile arrests are down in the last 5 years; teen birthrates are also down. Since 1995, college enrollments have increased.

196. Dark Skin Lesions

Dark skin lesions on the neck folds, armpits, and elbows may be an early indicator of risk for type II diabetes. Weight loss, a healthy diet, and exercise can ward off type II diabetes.

197. TVs Need Firm Hands

You can help mold a child's behavior by putting a firm hand on the TV control.

198. On Teaching Responsibility

On a family vacation, an eleven-year-old son purchased a pocketknife. The parents spelled out conditions under which he could use it. On the first rest stop, he threw the blade in the sand close to his brother's feet, calling himself "Chief Sharp Knife." The father pocketed the knife for the entire vacation. "Now you're Chief No-Knife," teased his brother. That experience taught the child more about responsibility than any scolding.

199. It Is Better to Light One Candle Than to Curse the Darkness

Don't worry and be anxious over the things you cannot change. On the other hand, when you can do something, however small, to help your child or anyone else, do it quickly and without expectation of something in return.

200. Love Unconditionally

Any child, no matter how incorrigible, should always feel that his parents love him UNCONDITIONALLY.

201. Try Always to Be Patient

As we recall God's patience toward us, we show growth in patience toward our children.

202. On Hating

It has often been said that hating people is like burning down the barn to get rid of the rats. It is much too costly, regardless of the reason.

203. Discussing Feelings and Problems

Older children need to feel free to discuss feelings and problems with parents. If parents are critical or seem shocked, children will either bottle up their feelings or take them elsewhere.

204. Can Having a Pet Really Help a Child?

Cats and dogs can be wonderful companions. They may satisfy the child's need to nurture and be nurtured. The birth of a kitten or the death of the family dog can be a valuable way to help children understand and cope with some of life's most fundamental issues.

205. How Much Sleep Does My Child Need?

How much sleep do kids actually require? Toddlers need about 10 to 13 hours a day (including a nap); kindergartners need between 10 to 12 hours. Children between the ages of 2 and 3 who sleep less than 10 hours during a 24-hour period are at risk for behavior problems, including noncompliance and aggression.

206. Television Isolates

When parents choose watching TV to a family activity, the family may be headed for trouble. TV tends to isolate, not unify, families.

207. Save Precious Time

Turn off your TV for 7 days. You will be amazed that you will have a lot more time to do things that you didn't think you would ever have a chance to do (like play with your children and read to them daily).

208. Memory Lapses Can Be Normal

Memory lapses are normal at any age. Be wary when the lapses are progressive and associated with personality changes. Don't worry if you can't find your car in the parking lot, but if you can't remember what kind of car you drive, you have a problem.

209. Max Out Your 401(K) Contribution

You won't see the cash until retirement, but it gives you the two things you need to become wealthy: compounded gains and annual tax deductions.

210. Be Assertive in the Emergency Room

Being assertive could save your life. Don't be too shy to do it.
Ask for a full explanation of any procedure that is being done. If there is a lag in emergency care, be demanding to the nurse in charge.

211. A Successful Marriage

It never occurs to the couple that they have compromised anything.

212. Rye Bread Is Good

Rye bread contains more fiber than any other bread. It helps lower cholesterol and triglycerides and may help your body process sugar. One study showed it reduced the risk of heart attacks by more than 15 percent. Baking with rye flour is also good.

213. Children Who "Just Will Not Eat"

Don't worry when your child "just will not eat." The observation that laboratory rats not only live longer, but also have fewer age-associated diseases when their food intake is restricted, dates back to the 1930s. Studies show that caloric restriction prolongs life in laboratory animals, evokes an array of responses, including a decrease in oxidative stress and damage, and may retard the aging process in humans.

214. Obesity Prediction

Among older children, obesity is an increasingly important predictor of adult obesity, regardless of whether the parents are obese. Parental obesity more than doubles the risk of adult obesity among both obese and non-obese children under 10 years of age.

215. Teach Budgeting When Appropriate

Tell kids about family finances in age-appropriate ways. Around age 5, children can understand that the family must earn money to buy what it needs. Try grocery shopping with kids, explaining the budget for that trip, then showing them how you use the money. By age 8 or 9, most children can understand that the family should put aside money for food, shelter, or doctor bills before spending on less important things.

216. Work With—Not Against—Your Child's Teacher

Here are ways to get along with your child's schoolteacher. Don't go to a meeting with a chip on your shoulder. See the conference as an opportunity to get a more objective view of how your child functions away from you. Saying something like "I know you want my child to have the most successful year possible" can break down barriers. Write down what the teacher is saying so you can remember the comments clearly and accurately. Taking notes also shows that you respect what the teacher is saying.

217. What Men Want for Fathers Day

1. More time with the family: 41%
2. To hang out with or talk to their own fathers: 13%
3. Something expensive: 10%
4. Good health for them and their family: 9%
5. A day off, or to sleep in, etc.: 9%

218. Don't Forget Seatbelts

It's amazing how some health-conscious people—folks who eat right, don't smoke and who would never miss a workout—decide that it's somehow okay not to wear seatbelts.

219. Help Your Children NOT to Be Cynical!

British medical journal *Lancet* found that people with cynical attitudes may be as much as 50 percent more likely to suffer a heart attack than more laid-back people. Cynics are less capable of accepting and benefiting from social encouragement.

220. The Virtue of Praise

Harriet Beecher Stowe wrote the famous book, *Uncle Tom's Cabin*. In the book, she extolled the virtue of praise. Most parents can find something that bolsters a child: "I appreciate your honesty." "Thanks for your help." "I like the way you make your bed." "You are getting better about...."

221. DO NOT SMOKE

Heed three simple words to guard your child against emphysema, heart trouble, lung disease, vascular problems, cancer, stroke, and the early loss of a parent: DO NOT SMOKE.

222. Oh, the Power of Words!

Which of these directions is given in a supportive manner?

"Make your bed this minute or you'll be sorry!"
    OR
"Will you please make your bed?"

223. Chicken Pox Vaccine Good for Shingles, Too

One of the important benefits of varicella vaccine is that shingles occurs 5-7 times less often after vaccination than after natural varicella.

224. Grandmother Was Wrong—for Once

Swallowing fruit pits or seeds does not cause acute appendicitis.

225. There Is an Increasing Frequency of Mastoiditis
This fact is due to antibiotic resistant bacteria that cause pneumonia.

226. Ear Implant for Deafness
The earlier the implantation, the better the outcome.
Seek an appointment with the pediatrician as soon as you detect a hearing problem in your child.

227. Humor Is Healthy
Laughter makes us healthier in at least five ways. It lowers blood pressure, slows the heart rate, reduces pain, boosts the immune system, and decreases the hormones that cause stress.

228. Want a Boy Baby?
1. Start young—Older parents are more likely to have girls.
2. Conceive in the summer—Heat kills more X-chromosomes (female), leaving the Y-chromosomes (male) free to dart around.

229. A Link between the Head and the Heart
Here are the facts comparing balding and non-balding men:
Frontal balding—9% more likely to have coronary heart disease.
Top balding—About 30% more likely to have coronary heart disease.

230. Office Work Should Be at the Office
Almost NEVER take office work home with you.

231. Where There Is One Defect, Look for Others
There is a high incidence of neurologic abnormalities in infants with congenital heart disease prior to surgical management.

232. Children and Chores

Does your child dawdle when doing chores? Try listing the chores on a chart. Give her a star (or one point) for every day chores are done promptly and well. For seven successful days, honor her at dinner with a special treat.

233. Listen, Listen, Listen

The simplest way to let a child know you love him is to give him your complete attention when he talks to you.

234. On Being Firm

A mother tells the following story:

No matter how supportive we were, our teenage son suffered emotionally from being uprooted from close friends and school in our family's move to another city. He, along with the other children, had weekly responsibilities. One Saturday it was his turn to clean the bathrooms. When they had not been done by early afternoon, I calmly reminded him he could not go on his date until they had been completed. Yet at six o'clock, the lad simply picked up the keys from my dresser and came downstairs, ready for his date. His chores were not done.

"Son," said I, in a calm voice, "if you go outside that door, I shall have to call the police."

"You wouldn't!" said he.

"I should hate to, but I will," I answered, calm outside but quivering within.

He rushed upstairs to call his date.

Relations were strained for a week or so, but there were no more problems over shared responsibilities in the home.

This son is now grown, an outstanding professional, a concerned citizen, and a devoted son. This Mother's Day, he wrote a letter saying, "Mom, I'm so very thankful that you held the line during my turbulent years."

235. Family as a Priority
Your child will make her family a priority only if she sees her parents doing so. Actions speak louder than words.

236. Complete Attention
Show love to your children by giving them your complete attention when needed. That casserole you need to make can wait a few minutes when it comes to the needs of your children.

237. Appear or Be Good?
Which do you really want for your child: to appear good or to be good?

238. To Do and Not to Do
Extreme permissiveness is bad. So is severe authoritarianism. Parents should see that children NOT do some things they would prefer to do, and do some things they would prefer NOT to do.

239. What Does a Child's Misbehavior Communicate to Parents?
1. Resistance to rigid parental control
2. Incapable of the work expected of him
3. Learning disability (attention deficit disorder)
4. Low self-esteem
5. Learning needs unmet
6. Frustration with sibling competition

240. Drugs for Depression

The average man likely will suffer from depression at some point in his life. However, there are twice as many drugs written for women with depression as there are for men with depression.

241. Another Reason Not to Smoke

1. The average male will lose 5.4 teeth by age 72.
2. Males who smoke will lose 12 teeth by age 72.

242. If Your Marriage Is "Slowing Down," Try These Moves

A group of women were asked, "Which of the following spontaneous gestures do you find romantic?" These percentages give surprising answers.

A hidden note: 41%
A bouquet of flowers: 28%
A surprise date: 10%
A greeting card: 7%
Jewelry: 6%

243. Global Fat—a Big Problem

The percentage of obese Americans is 35 percent and increasing, but Europe is not far behind. An International Obesity Task Force reports that 15 to 20 percent of Europeans are obese. The rate is highest in Eastern Europe, rising to 50 percent among some women, and lowest in Scandinavia and the Netherlands, where slender people are still the norm. Even in poorer nations such as China and parts of South America, people are getting fatter faster. Are they getting more TVs?

244. All Three Types of Tea Come from the SAME LEAF

The difference lies in how they are processed:

1. Black teas—the preferred drink in Europe and the Americas—are partially dried, crushed, allowed to "ferment" or oxidize in heat for a few hours, and then fully dried.
2. Oolong teas, or red teas, are also oxidized, but for a shorter time.
3. Green teas, the preferred drink in Asia, are not crushed and oxidized. Instead, they are steamed, and then rolled and dried.

245. Olives and Avocados
Olives and avocados are the only fruits high in fat, though the fat is mostly mono-unsaturated.

246. Cars Are Not Rights
It isn't in the Bill of Rights that a child gets a car when he is 16 years of age.

247. Cars and Drivers Increasing
Since 1969 the number of motor vehicles in the U.S. has grown twice as fast as the number of drivers and six times faster than the human population, according to the government's Nationwide Personal Transportation Survey. Here are more data:

Increase in drivers since 1969: more than 70 percent
Increase in vehicles: 145 percent

248. Teen Parties
Parties for teens: Limit the party to one area of the house—the patio or the den—so you can keep an eye on things. Make sure there are plenty of food, alcohol-free drinks, and music. Tell the police about the party so they can drive by. Walk in and out of the scene yourself every 15 to 20 minutes. To keep the kids busy, enlist their help in preparing and serving the food.

249. Vaginal Discharge in Children
If a girl is coming in for a vaginal discharge exam, do not bathe her the night before. Also bring along the last pair of panties that were stained.

250. Confidentiality Ends with Abuse

Physician confidentiality ends when a patient places himself or others in danger or in situations of physical or sexual abuse.

251. Energy from Vitamins?

There is no vitamin that is a source of energy.

252. Religion and Mortality

Among 200 patients undergoing open-heart surgery, "those without any strength or comfort from religion had almost three times the risk of death," according to researchers at the Dartmouth Medical School, Lebanon, NH. Participation in any kind of organized group improved survival rates, but the more religious the patients, the better they fared. All of the 37 patients who described themselves as "deeply religious" survived.

253. Social Rejection

Help children realize that social rejection is a normal part of life and they cannot control initial rejection. They can, however, control their response to it. Acknowledge kids' hurt feelings, and then ask them what they think they can do better to be able to join in.

254. Praise Work—Not Ability

Praise kids for working hard—not for their natural abilities. Telling a child he is smart makes it harder for him to handle mistakes—he may think he is no longer smart if he makes mistakes. But telling children that they did well because they worked hard encourages them to work even harder to fix errors.

255. Children Need to Taste

Children may need to taste a food eight to ten times before they accept it. To get young kids to eat right, serve a variety of food; let the kids see you eating different foods.

256. No Two Children Are Alike

A speaker was lecturing on Proverbs 22:6: "Train up a child in the way he should go." The speaker outlined the same training for children in the home, regardless of their strengths and weaknesses or temperaments. One of his listeners commented, "No two children can ever fit into the same mold. That's what makes parenting a stimulating and rewarding adventure. Value the basic nature of each child and adapt sensibly to it."

257. Define Boundaries

A fence is of little use in cultivating secure feelings in a child unless she knows the exact boundaries of that fence.

258. Basic Guidelines for All Family Members

NEVER use threats as a means of control. And remember that everyone needs to feel appreciated.

259. How a Child Sees Herself

A child's opinion of herself is influenced by her parents more than by any other person or thing.

260. Tone of Voice

What tone of voice do you most often use with your children? Consider this little poem,

"Come here!" I sharply ordered;
And a child cowered and wept.
"Come here," I softly whispered;
And into my arms he crept.

261. Two Kinds of Behavior

Don't stew too much over behavior that a child will soon outgrow. Save the stewing for behavior that will have lasting consequences.

262. The Wonder of the Christmas Season

As a family project, decorate the tree, fireplace, and other areas. Children will engage more readily in worship around settings they have helped to make. Gather the entire family daily for short periods around one of these centers of interest. Tell or read portions from Matthew 1-2 and Luke 2. Then talk about the real meaning of Christmas.

263. Keep the Past in the Past

Work to keep the past in the past. Grieve it and let it go. Reduce the size of your "rear-view mirror."

264. Many Drugs Not Tested in Children

Only 40 percent of drugs widely used in pediatric populations have been actually tested on children.

265. What Did You Say?

The average male loses about 6% of his hearing every 10 years! Cut down that car stereo!

266. Pets May Be Good

In a 1980 study of patients who returned home after heart attacks, only 6 percent of those with pets died, while 44 percent of those without pets suffered a fatal relapse. Elderly pet owners reported fewer doctor visits than non-pet owners in a 1990 survey.

267. Guys Are Twice as Likely to Die in an Auto Accident As Women

There are at least three reasons for this:

　1. Men drive faster than women.

2. They don't wear their seat belts as much as women.

3. They will not let a woman who is drinking get behind the wheel.

268. Be Courteous

Be polite and courteous. It costs nothing to acquire and practice courtesy.

269. Share Burdens

Don't keep it inside: Talk things over with someone you trust. Talk to your mate or a friend. "A burden shared is half a burden."

270. Understanding Blind People

Whether or not you have a blind person in your neighborhood, help children understand a blind person's problems. One way to do it is to provide a blindfold for each child in the home. Avoiding danger areas, give each one several tasks that require mobility. At the end, encourage them to talk about their feelings. Later, perhaps around the dinner table, read and discuss the biblical story of Bartimaeus (Mark 10:46-52). Or, if you prefer, get a library copy of Helen Keller's life and relate a fitting incident about her. Encourage children to be thankful for the wonderful gift of sight.

271. On Genuine Forgiveness

Two sons, a teenager and a spirited eight-year-old, had a heated argument. Later, the teenager tried without success to get his brother to accept his apology. Finally, the father tried at length to get the boy to forgive his brother. At last the eight-year-old agreed, adding, "But I'll say it in a sarcastic way!"

Use this incident as a springboard for similar problems in your family that call for a genuinely forgiving spirit.

272. Firm Voice of Authority

Although children are not aware of it, they want the gentle but firm voice of authority.

273. Saying "I'm Sorry"

Children who squabble often can learn that sincerely saying "I'm sorry" is a wonderful starting point for making things right. But do not forget to practice what you preach. When you err, you need to make things right with your children.

274. Always Eat Breakfast

Children who eat breakfast regularly do better in school. They tend to think faster and more clearly, and they solve classroom problems more easily.

275. Limit Television Watching

A woman related the incident of a family who bought a weekly TV Guide. The family decided what they would watch that week, limiting daily viewing to about an hour. A better suggestion would have been to lower the time to one hour three times a week only. There are few things today that damage your child more, aside from heavy use of drugs.

276. Some "Whens" for Parents to Consider

When to tighten the reins and when to slacken them;
When to admonish and when to praise;
When to call the doctor and when to use common sense;
When to lend an ear and when to talk;
When to push and when to hold off;
When to let the child try his wings and when to say, "Wait a bit."

277. Laughter Makes Everybody Feel Better

Every child needs a parent who laughs and smiles a lot.

278. Are You Tuned In?

Parents are too busy who are not tuned in enough to children to know when they need to be encouraged.

279. Let Bygones Be Bygones

One of the most important things for each of us to learn and to live is to forgive and let the past remain in the past. Do you tend to hold grudges?

280. How Do You Use Power in Your Relationships?

As parents, your job is filled with astounding power. Use it wisely.

281. Check Out Your Child's Friends

Children mimic the habits of close friends. Actively seek the right kind for your child. You have more mature judgment and can in secret get the task accomplished. No child should visit a friend's home where no adult is present.

282. Help Your Child Develop His Natural Abilities

He was just an average boy who liked airplanes. That's all he drew in his spare time. Teachers took little notice. When grown, he went into the Air Force. Years later this boy, Dick Scobee, became Commander of the space shuttle Challenger.

283. Prayer Is a Powerful Resource

When all else fail fails to reach deeply troubled children, parents and teachers still have one powerful recourse: prayer. "More things are wrought by prayer than this world dreams of." Tennyson

284. Children Become Less Pliable with Each Passing Year

If parents wait until a child starts to school to discipline him, they'll likely have little success or find that remediation of their error will be a long, tough process.

285. Stay Healthy for Your Grandchildren

Odds that the average man will have a heart attack are 1 in 21. Odds that the average man will develop heart disease before age 60 are 1 in 3. The best prevention, of course, results from stuff you already know about: Exercise and keep your fat intake below 30 percent of your total calories. DO NOT SMOKE.

286. Here Are Some Averages: Mostly Bad!

1. The average male drinks 3.3 cups of coffee per day.
2. He eats 1.5 servings of fruit. He should eat 4.
3. The average male is 30 pounds overweight.
4. The average married male eats much less fat and more vegetables than a single man. The latter has no wife to cook for him.
5. The average male has 1.2 alcoholic drinks per day.

287. On Giving Children Some Voice

John, a first grader, had a bad fall. The mother cleaned the wounds but met with resistance when she tried to apply alcohol. She said, "If necessary, we'll hold you down and apply it."

John sobbed, "OK, but first let me go to my room and pray!"

The family was not sure how much praying he did. More important, the boy felt he had been given some voice in the decision.

288. You Be the Judge

Which of these is good discipline and which is cruelty?

• Ignoring unacceptable behavior until the child forms a habit of defiance.

- Firmly checking strong-willed tendencies before misbehavior becomes entrenched.

289. One of the Greatest Gifts You Can Give Your Children
Look for the best in your children, and give them your best.

290. When Your Child Asks You to Read or Play...
When you're busy and your child asks you to read to her or play with her, which is your more common response:
"Not now, dear. I must get supper."
"Sure. I can take a ten-minute break."

291. Some Rules for Raising Nice Children
1. Help your child feel secure and loved.
2. Set limits on what your children are allowed to do so that they know what's expected of them and what will happen if the rules are broken. Instead of making too many rules, make a few that can be enforced.
3. Impose on them that winning isn't everything, but doing their best is!
4. Set challenging goals, but make them realistic and attainable.
5. Encourage children to express their feelings. Good communication is very important.
6. Be supportive of your children's creativity and don't be too quick to criticize. Allow children to feel good about expressing themselves through drawing, painting, and writing.

292. Mashed Fingernails
If you mash your fingernail, immediately squeeze the fingertip and keep pressure on it for 5 minutes. Icing can help. These measures decrease internal bleeding and swelling, which can displace the nail root from its bed.

293. Why Are Brand Name Drugs So Expensive?
Millions more dollars are spent on advertising and promotion than on research.

294. Predicting Obesity
The probability of being obese as a young adult increases with the age of the obese child and is higher at all ages for the group of very obese children.

After six years of age, the probability of obesity in adulthood exceeds 50 percent for obese children, as compared with about 10 percent for non-obese children. Obesity at one or two years of age is not associated with an increased risk of adult obesity.

Overall, there is no significant difference between the sexes in the risk of adult obesity associated with childhood obesity. The risk of adult obesity is significantly greater if either the mother or the father is obese. There are no significant differences in these risk estimates between boys and girls.

295. Be Careful with Your Doses
In one study, only one-third of the parents correctly identified a teaspoon (5cc). Sixty percent erroneously identified a tablespoon (three times the dose of a teaspoon).

296. Conflicts Don't Take Holidays
Don't expect family conflicts to go away suddenly during any holiday season. If fact, many people find the holidays to be especially stressful.

297. Sunday School and Church
If parents don't think that Sunday school and church are important, when their children reach adulthood it is unlikely that their children will attend church, either. The apple doesn't fall far from the tree.

298. Cooked Shrimp

If the shrimp have been cooked, eating the "vein" won't hurt you.

299. How to Help Your Kids Stay Close

Give them their space—TOGETHER.

300. How to Save a Knocked Out Tooth

The faster a tooth can be reinserted into its socket, the more likely it will reattach itself and continue to grow. If the tooth is replaced in its socket within 30 minutes, there is a 70 percent chance it will reattach successfully. Chances decrease to 40 percent after 30 to 90 minutes. While you're in route for medical help, it's important to keep the tooth moist, but don't put it in water for the trip. Water draws the nutrients and calcium out of the tooth.

301. Get Rid of Molds

Diluted chlorine bleach is the best agent to destroy surface mold for allergic patients.

302. Parents and Children Do Not Take in All the Doctor Says

Physicians overestimate the extent to which patients "take in" instructions. The parent and/or the child should repeat the instructions to make sure that they are understood.

303. Cold Packs Are Right at Home

If you need a cold pack for a burn, look in the refrigerator and get a frozen bag of meat or vegetables. Apply it to the burn.

304. Home Health Care

Health care given in the home is the most effective way to deliver most health care today.

305. Why Is My Child "Slow" in School?
Reading difficulty is by far the most widespread and potentially damaging learning disability. Reading difficulties are usually lifelong.

306. TV Can Be Good (Educational) OR Bad (Nudity, Violence, Etc.)
Supervision of the child's TV viewing is the parent's responsibility. Most children watch too much (4 hours + daily) with too little supervision. Parents should be selective in what they watch and set a good example for the children (Dad doesn't need to watch football all weekend).

307. Why Is Johnny So Defiant?
When parents complain about a young child's oppositional and defiant behavior, disorders of attention and learning should head the list of diagnoses to be considered. Faced with the requirement to accomplish tasks that they cannot perform, most children would prefer to say, "I won't," rather than, "I can't," because the former allows a greater semblance of control.

308. What a Shock
Never touch a victim of electrical shock until you know that the electrical contact is broken.

309. Managed Care and Merger Mania
Some consolidations are motivated not so much by a search for efficiency as by a desire for market power—power that can force lower prices for everything the organization buys and higher prices for what it sells. This market power may be good for the organization's bottom line, but it is of questionable value to society.

310. A Fitting Prayer for Parents at Each Day's Beginning
Help me to teach my children to be compassionate and tolerant, and to stand for what is right at all times.

311. Learn to Forget
Yesterday is gone forever. Forget it. Today is brand new. Move on!

312. Send the Right Signals
Every child needs to feel she's important. When a phone call can delay dinner preparation for several minutes and a child cannot do so, you're sending the wrong signals.

313. You Choose What to Do with Your Time
A teacher advised a mother to spend time with her children. "I don't have time," she replied, recounting numerous responsibilities.

"Be honest," said the teacher. "Do you watch TV for an hour on most days?"

"Well, yea," she stuttered. Before she could excuse herself, the teacher replied, "Then you do have time."

314. Burns and Blister
See a doctor for a large burn that covers more than one square inch anywhere on your child's body. See a doctor for any burn, no matter what size, on the hands, feet, face, or genitals. Let blisters pop on their own.

315. Don't Give a Lot of Anti-Diarrhea Medicine for Diarrhea
The diarrhea itself is probably not a problem. Anti-diarrhea medicine for kids is not the solution because if the diarrhea is being caused by a bacteria, that's the body's way of getting rid of it. If you stop the diarrhea, the bacteria are still in there. Your main worry is dehydration.

316. Irrigate Cuts and Wounds with Water
Hydrogen peroxide may damage the skin and actually interfere with healing. Get rid of dirt, germs and debris by irrigating with water.

317. Bee Stings—Stay Calm! Get an Adrenaline Shot—Fast!
See a doctor for any systemic symptoms of an allergic reaction (difficulty breathing or swallowing, hives, vomiting, weakness, dizziness, nausea, swelling: these typically occur within a few minutes of the sting).

318. God's Love
When we love others, we simply are letting God's love operate in us.

319. Check Temptations to be Rude
"Rudeness is the weak man' s imitation of strength." Eric Hoffer

320. Teenagers Pay Their Own Fines
If a teenager is caught speeding he should pay the fine. He has no money? Ask someone to hire him for odd jobs. Secretly reimburse that friend. After the youngster finally pays the fine, he may never again get a speeding ticket.

321. An Old Adage
"Do not squander time, for it is the stuff life is made of." Memorization is a lost art. Teach your children sayings that will stick with them through life.

322. Another Good Quote
A good quotation to discuss at the dinner table when twelve-year-olds and older are present: "You can preach a better sermon with your life than with your lips." Oliver Goldsmith

323. Small Things Are Important
Recognize the small things your kids do. You not only will please them, but you'll stimulate love in their hearts.

324. Let Children See You Reading

To help children become good readers, let them, even as toddlers, see YOU engrossed in books. Read to them daily. Tell them bedtime stories. Stack the coffee table with books of all levels. Yard sales display unusual bargains. Choose carefully.

325. Rein in Television

Unless you would trust your children's mental and moral growth to a scalawag, don't give them free reins with the tube.

326. Destroying a Child's Self-Image

One of the most devastating ways to destroy a child's self-esteem is to shame him: "You look ridiculous in that outfit!" If that doesn't work, try name-calling: "Lazy bum, clean your trashy room immediately!" Some children either never get over such treatment or struggle for years to recover from the slaughter.

327. Time with Children

Children grasp your love by what you do WITH them, not FOR THEM. Too busy? Keep a daily chart for one week of time spent for sleep, work, TV, etc. Be thorough. Include time spent with each child.

328. Ways to Show Love

Your children know you love them only if you express it in ways they understand. Make them feel they come first. Show that you value their ideas. Really listen sympathetically. Find ways to communicate. Arrange frequent times together.

329. Wise Advice to Teenagers on Smoking

Don't dwell on the long-term effects of smoking to teenagers. Make it short!

　　1. You will smell bad.

2. Smoking is illegal under 18 years.

3. Smoking is an expensive habit.

4. Smoking may burn holes in your clothes.

5. Smoking will limit your physical fitness, especially in sports.

6. If you kiss someone, you will taste like an ashtray.

7. The majority of girls don't like to date a boy who smokes.

8. Frequently you must hide from parents when you do it.

9. Smoking is the gateway to all drug use!

Teenagers will not relate to the 40-to-50 year effects of cancer, strokes, heart trouble, and emphysema.

330. New Treatments
After a medical advance, it takes 8-10 years to change the way doctors practice. About 1300 medical articles are published per day. You can't keep up!

331. Death and Loss
Children of ages 10-12 have begun to grasp death. They have begun to grasp that it can strike anyone unexpectedly. They are also able to contemplate it in more abstract and universal ways. By age 12, children can talk about the spirit living on, and about the contributions someone made.

332. Love Is Eternal
A young friend saw the wedding picture of a couple, returned to the den with the picture, and asked in all seriousness: "If both of you knew then what you would look like now, would you have married each other?" What an opportunity to teach that love is eternal!

333. How to Achieve
"The three great essentials to achieve anything worthwhile are hard work, stick-to-itiveness, and common sense." Thomas A. Edison

334. Getting Even
Teach your children that the only people they should want to get even with are those who have helped them and been nice to them.

335. Dwelling on Lost Yesterdays
A good starting point for the day is Philippians 3:13: "Forgetting what is behind and straining toward what is ahead, I press on." Too many parents ruin what could be a happy day and jeopardize tomorrow by dwelling on a lost yesterday.

336. Does It Make Any Difference How a Child Is Dressed?
Yes! The first impression of a person is made on how he or she is dressed. I'm not saying we should be quickly judgmental, but we are; and so are our children. Remember, our children are passing judgment on us just the way we pass judgment on others. Your children are representing you and your family in the community **DAILY!**

337. A Profound Question
Is a life spent making a better gadget greater and more important than a life that is spent making a child into a man or woman? Mom, you have no higher honor or duty than choosing the latter!

338. I Can't Get My Child to Bed at Night
After age 2, frequent long afternoon naps may make your child a poor night sleeper.

339. Why Bribery Backfires
"Clean your room and you may watch TV," Mom stated. On the surface, both the parent and the child got what they wanted. The use of a reward unrelated to cleaning up motivated the child to watch television, not to clean her room. The child learned nothing that would inspire her to keep her room neat in the future. Instead, she discovered that resisting her

mother's requests would probably get her more television time. The mom did what all parents sometimes do: She bribed her child. With a little more forethought, she could have said, "Clean up your room now and you'll be able to find that book you were looking for." By so doing, she would have given her daughter a powerful motivation. The child would have realized that when she cleans her room, she knows where her things are.

340. Will the Family Enjoy It?
Rent camping equipment before buying if you are not sure what gear you need or whether your family will think camping is fun.

341. Make the Most of a "Teachable Moment"
When your child asks about some sexual act or saying on TV, take some time then to explain things. Don't say "We'll talk about that later" or "Your daddy will tell you about it." Explain it immediately!

342. Child Learns Best When He Pays for His Mistakes
Children should be given a fair amount of freedom. But sometimes freedom results in careless, destructive behavior unless it is balanced with high expectations, lots of responsibility, and the understanding that the child in question will be held accountable for the decisions he makes.

The majority of today's parents fall into one of two categories (1) parents who try to control what they can't and (2) parents who fail to control what they can. As a consequence, too many of today's children are lacking responsible self-control.

343. Anyway You Do it, Exercise Is Good
Three 10-minute bouts of jogging are as effective for improving fitness as a single 30-minute jog.

344. What Really Matters

1. Teaching children about values, manner, religion, and responsibility.
2. Helping a child to choose the right peers.
3. Practicing patience, not punishment.
4. Understanding the child's individuality and being flexible.

345. The Simple Life

A doctor was talking with an old lady recently who lived far out in the country. He asked about her husband Jim and how he was doing. She said, "Well, I'm not sure. About 4 weeks ago, he just 'woke up dead!'"

346. On Being Fully Present

A teacher told a mother she should spend time with her children. "Oh, I do," she said. "We watch TV every single night. About half the time, I read the paper, but I'm right there with the children."

"Do you choose which channels to watch?" asked the teacher. "Heaven, no!" she said. "We really would have a row!"

Simply being present in a room has no relation to sharing a child's thoughts and feelings any more so than the dog that lies at the child's feet might share the child's thoughts and feelings.

347. Bad Habits

Someone once said, "Bad habits are like a comfortable bed—easy to get into, but hard to get out of."

348. Children and Family Decisions

Do you invite your children to participate in making family decisions? Children whose opinions matter to parents are more likely to develop a strong sense of self-respect.

349. Five Things Your Child Isn't Learning in Many Schools

1. Memorization: It's a great exercise for your brain.
2. Cursive Writing: Many teachers are not trained to teach this.
3. Study skills: Some teachers neglect thorough instruction in study skills.
4. Heroes: Role models who exhibit courage, honor, and virtue become part of a child's subconscious self.
5. Writing skills: Children need to be taught the art of creating, outlining, and revising stories and themes.

350. To Thine Own Self...

Shakespeare said, "This above all: to thine own self be true, And it must follow, as the night the day, Thou canst not then be false to any man."

351. Each Day Saturate Your Mind with Proverbs

"A cheerful heart is good medicine, but a crushed spirit dries up the bones." (Proverbs 17:22) But watch out if you have children: a merry heart is contagious!

352. Rage Ages

This old familiar saying is very apt for parents: "The people who always seem young are those who will never reveal their rage."

353. Might Is a Poor Technique for Discipline

"Shut your mouth! You'll obey me because I said so!" No one can respond positively to such commands.

354. Needed: Adult Role Models

A generation or more ago, children usually had instant access to several adult role models: grandparents, cousins, in-laws, and neighbors. Now their role models are most often peer groups. Parents should explore the neighborhood, work place, or church groups with the intention of forming a few close family friendships with adults who have solid value systems. Then perhaps their children, if hesitant to confront parents with certain problems, will turn to one of these adults for guidance and perhaps bypass the immature advice of peer groups.

355. Respect Goes Two Ways

If we want our children to respect us, we must act in respectable ways. Acting respectably does not include screaming at children or physically abusing them. Regarding physical abuse, there's a big difference between physical abuse and occasionally slapping a child's arm or giving him a few spanks on the bottom and then hugging him until his tears cease. The latter emanates from a deep love for the child. The former stems from a misguided view of parental authority.

356. Children Have Big Ears!

How Mom and Dad talk to each other as they travel to church may impact the children more than what they learn at church.

357. Teenagers Are "Raring to Go"

Capitalize on diverting this tremendous physical energy in acceptable ways: part-time jobs, music, sports, community service. Investigate every avenue in your community and subtly encourage your teenagers to get involved.

358. Guilt Is a Dreadful Means of Attempting to Control

"Why did you do this to me after all I've done for you?"
"Because of what you did, I had a splitting headache all night long!"

359. Two-Step Directions
Generally, children under seven or eight years of age should not be given more than two-step directions: "Change your shoes and then take the dog for a walk."

360. Focus on Moral Consequences
Parents of teenagers should be keenly aware of glandular changes that occur in these youngster's bodies. This gives parents no excuse to forfeit any effort to discipline. But it might be wise to center for the most part on breaches of conduct that have significant moral consequences.

361. The Highest Aims of Parenthood
If amid all the chores that come daily as parents you can give each child a deep sense that he belongs, he's understood, and he's loved, you will have achieved the highest aims of good parenthood.

362. Public Humiliation
An enraged parent punished a child in the throes of a tantrum. She slapped her hard on both cheeks, ranted at her, then slapped her again. Ten or twelve startled families waited behind her in the grocery line.

Cruel physical punishment can damage any child physically, but more lasting are the scars of being humiliated before others.

363. Parents: Apologize, Too
Be quick to tell your child you are sorry when hindsight has revealed your error in judgment. A sincere apology to your child will elevate you in her eyes, not lower you.

364. Foundations Are Crumbling
In a world where once-sturdy foundations are crumbling, we need builders: parents who will take on the challenge of resetting these

foundations for today's children with the building blocks of guidance, love, and gentle but firm discipline.

365. Things That Matter

A parent's daily challenge: to keep focused on the things that matter and give the other things only a fleeting glance.

366. Nobody's Business

In so far as it is possible, all reprimands to children should be made in private.

367. A Warning Sign

Some family members fall into the habit of putting down one another. Arrange a family conference to set some behavior goals that will build up one another.

368. Let Your Child Know Why

Let your child learn that "No" means "No," but briefly explain the reason for your decision.

369. On Dangerous Behavior

When a child is doing a dangerous thing, pain is a powerful persuader. A three-year-old put his little shoes in the chain link fence and climbed over it into the adjacent street. He had been warned about leaving the yard. The mother spanked his little bottom soundly, and he cried a bit on her shoulder. The mother caressed and kissed him and sent him right back into the enclosure. He never again climbed that fence.

We rarely suggest spanking a child but if he endangers himself or others with his behavior it may be necessary, as in the above case.

370. Adjust Allowances for Work Done Pleasantly

Are you uncertain about the whole subject of allowances? Try this method. Say: "I will pay you the full amount of your allowance if all chores are done completely, promptly, without grumbling, and if you are pleasant in helping out in other ways when called upon. But if any chores are not completed for the week, and when you are not pleasant in helping out in other ways, your allowance will be cut in half." This method mirrors what happens in the real world when adults do poor work on the job.

371. A Most Precious Investment

The untaxable dividends you make are the investments of time you spend with your children.

372. Who Nurtures Your Child?

A child's progress is in direct relation to the persons under whose influence he lives.

373. Can Parents Overdo the Praise Bit?

You bet! Parents who praise for every small thing teach children to expect it constantly. Praise often but not profusely.

374. Trusting Versus Excessive Concern…A Fine Line

Do you excessively remind your teenagers to drive carefully, stay out of trouble, lock the car, keep within speed limits, and so forth? They like to think they can handle a few things. Walk the fine line between being excessively concerned and trusting your teenager.

375. A Practical Matter

Finding extra time to listen to your child is easier than making the child resentful by your not doing so.

376. Gifts from the Lord

Psalm 127: 3-4 and Proverbs 23:24-25 say children are a "gift from the Lord" and we should "delight in them." Delight in the fact that they are active creatures and arrange multiple activities that foster family togetherness.

377. Fear of the Dark

Do not scold a child who is afraid of the dark. Put a night light in her room and leave the door open. Be patient until her fear goes away.

378. Lock Up Matches

If you keep matches or cigarette lighters in the home, put them out of children's reach, preferably under lock and key. And if you smoke, STOP.

379. Love from God

Many experts on child rearing emphasize that parents need to instill in children a firm faith in Jesus Christ. From birth onward, they should see their parents live out this faith. Surround your children with the love that emanates from God Himself. When their faith blossoms, it will reflect your own.

380. Dealing with Offensive Friends

Remember the saying, "One rotten apple spoils the whole basket." Invite your child's friends to your home. If a friend behaves in an offensive way, do not disparage the child, but greatly lessen his association with your child in the future.

381. Defining Time with Your Children

Often we read statements like "I don't get to be with my children often, but when I do, I make sure it's quality time." That philosophy is like a half-baked cake. Quality time can benefit children only if it's in a quantity-time framework. That parent may need to shut off the TV, discontinue the paper, take the receiver off the telephone, and cut out a club activity until the needs of her children truly become her first priority. No, it isn't easy. But the dividends are worth it.

382. Disciplining Toddlers

Parents who don't discipline during the toddler years often find that the child has "toddled" beyond their power to discipline him later.

383. Smiles Are Contagious

Sad children—yours or someone else's—are a common sight these days. Your smile might lessen the gloom in a sad child's heart.

384. Older Children's Friends

Older children who know they are loved and appreciated will be less likely to seek acceptance within unwholesome groups.

385. Tell Children When You Will Return

If you leave your child at a daycare center or with a sitter, lessen the child's fears by giving her an idea when you'll return. Also, let her know where she can reach you.

386. Who Comes First for You?

Practice the habit of tuning in to your children. Listen thoughtfully to what they say, think, and feel.

387. Grandparents Are Needed

A four-year-old grandson visited his grandparents for a week. He threw a huge tantrum when it was time to leave. The grandmother picked him up and soundly spanked him on the outer edges of his buttocks. The little boy hugged her neck and sobbed.

"Grandma loves you," the grandmother said, "but you can't act that way here." They exchanged kisses and the little fellow was happy for the three-hour drive home. The grandmother now remembers after twenty-one years the sense of security that was evident in the little fellow during that ride. This leads one to believe grandparents should utilize their years of experience in impacting young children's lives when possible.

388. Acceptance Is Essential
If you love your child as he is now, he'll find it easier to grow into the person he needs to be.

389. Why Did My Baby Die?
You might find it helpful to contact ASIDSI in order better to understand why some infants die for no apparent reason. This organization is a group of health-care professionals, researchers, and laypeople concerned about sudden infant death syndrome (SIDS), as well as families who have lost babies to SIDS, who work to identify the cause and cure of SIDS. The institute conducts research on the siblings of SIDS babies and promotes infant health through research, clinical services, and education.

American Sudden Infant Death Syndrome Institute (ASIDSI)
(Also known as American SIDS Institute)
6065 Roswell Rd., Suite 876
Atlanta, GA 30328
Phone: (404) 843-1030
Toll-free: (800) 232-SIDS
Fax: (404) 843-0577

390. Rules for Chores
Establish a firm rule that chores are to be done before viewing TV, inviting friends over for inside or outside play, telephone use, or computer use.

Parents should decide whether homework comes before chores. Some children do homework better immediately after returning from school.

391. Throwing Rocks at Cars Is Dangerous!

Throwing rocks at cars comes under the category of "Dangerous!" This is not the time for "If you do that again...." Spank the child soundly. Briefly describe the danger involved. Then love him and let the matter rest.
If the child is too old to spank, use other firm forms of discipline.

392. You Never Know Who Is Listening

Be careful what you discuss over a cordless phone. Such phones broadcast over an unlicensed frequency band shared with numerous other radio-operated devices.

393. How to Handle a Rude Person

Smile your biggest smile and make eye contact. Then softly and firmly voice your request.

394. House Rules at Home or Away from Home

1. Show respect—every person is important.
2. Speak for yourself—not for anybody else.
3. Listen to others—then they'll listen to you.
4. Avoid put-downs—who needs them?

395. Another Good Reason to Attend Religious Services

People who go to religious services with some regularity live longer than those who don't.

396. A Painless Removal Of Tape

To make removing a bandage almost ouchless (especially if it's on tender or hairy skin): Rub a cotton ball saturated with rubbing alcohol over the bandage. Alcohol loosens the adhesive, so the bandage will come off with less pull and pain. It works on adults, too!

397. Seven Cancer-Fighting Foods:

1. Broccoli
2. Tomatoes
3. Spinach
4. Oranges
5. Garlic
6. Apples
7. Soybeans

398. What Are Some Signs and Symptoms of STRESS in Your Children?

The answer to this question depends on the age of the child. A preschooler may regress in his behavior. School-age children may develop a variety of behavior problems. In kids of all ages, stress can trigger physical ailments such as headaches, stomachaches, sleeplessness, and emotional problems such as extreme shyness and withdrawal from family members.

399. Pancake Syrup instead of Butter

One tablespoon of pancake syrup has about 50 calories and no fat; "light" syrup has about 25 calories. Butter, however, has 100 calories per tablespoon and can be pure fat.

400. Don't Use Hanging Pest Strips

These strips constantly release pesticide into the air you breathe.

401. Another Reason to Exercise

Brief workouts (10 to 20 minutes) reduce the feeling of sadness, tension, fatigue, anger, and confusion. And they are free!

402. Learn At Museums

When you go to different cities, museums should be at the top of your list for places to take your children. The Cumberland Museum in Nashville is a good example of this.

403. Join the YMCA

For healthy life styles, join the YMCA. Exercise is a great focus for you and your family. Make it a habit.

Also, with its after-school programs, the YMCA takes care of more children daily than any other organization.

404. The Greatest Vocation

Parents are involved in one of the greatest vocations: shapers of young lives. This is worthy of their best efforts.

405. Laughter Is a Wonderful Tonic!

A mother told this story: Seeing the humor in a situation can help parents keep the balance.

"My small son, while sitting on my lap in church, asked to go to the restroom. Since I had taken him earlier, I denied his request. He turned his innocent-looking eyes up to me and said, 'You wouldn't want me to wet my pants, would you?' A bit of diplomacy rather than a tantrum paid off! My compliance seemed to do no lasting harm, for he is now a fine, sensitive editor of a newspaper."

406. Discipline for Teenagers

Parents who can discipline teenagers without anger have taken a giant step in the right direction.

407. Children Pay for Their Mistakes

Your child has been told not to play ball in a neighbor's yard. Yet he does so, and breaks a window. Allowances should be stopped or cut sharply until the child pays for the repair job. This does the child more good than scolding.

408. It's Illegal

Thirty-six percent of Tennessee high school students and fourteen percent of middle-school students are current smokers. That's compared to twenty-six percent of Tennessee adults. Cigarettes are illegal for kids to buy or smoke, but they're still smoking them at higher rates than adults do.

409. For the Mouth You Love to Kiss

To improve your breath, gently brush your tongue when you brush your teeth. That will help remove odor-causing bacteria lodged on the surface of the tongue, particularly toward the rear of your mouth.

GOOD RESOURCES AND ORGANIZATIONS
Adoptive Families of America
3333 Highway 100 North
Minneapolis, MN 55422
800-372-3330

National Adoption Information Clearing House
P O Box 1182
Washington, DC 20013-1182
703-246-9095

International Adoption Clinic
University of Minnesota
Box 211, UMHC
420 Delaware Street SE

Minneapolis, MN 55455
612-626-0644

International Adoption Clinic
The Floating Hospital
Boston, MA 02111
617-636-8121

NATIONAL ORGANIZATION OF MOTHERS OF TWINS CLUBS
PO Box 23188
Albuquerque, NM 87192-1188
Phone: (505) 275-0955 (business office)
Toll-free: (800) 275-0955 (referrals and brochures only)
Fax: (505) 296-1863
Email: NOMOTC@aol.com
Website: www. Nomotc.org
Description: The National Organization of Mothers of Twins Clubs
(NOMOTC) is a national network of local clubs focusing on research
and education.

PRINTED RESOURCES
Raising Compassionate, Courageous Children in a Violent World
(Longstreet Press) by Janice Cohn, Ph.D.

Raising Good Children: From Birth Through the Teenage Years (Bantam)
by Thomas Lickona, Ph.D.

An Indexed Guide
(Numbers refer to Numbered Pearls)

Preparation for Parenting

In addition to the following entries, this book includes other ones as preparation for parenting. Among them are the sections, "Pearls of Wisdom" and "Random Reflections." These entries are to enrich parents' personal lives, equipping them to be better parents of children of all ages.

Parenting for ALL Ages

Allowances

Health and safety

value of buttermilk, 6
of rye bread, 212
of tomatoes, 39
watching calories, 28, 399

exercise

advantages, 56, 156, 157, 401
benefits of YMCA, 403
drying exercise shoes, 40
need for relaxation, 7
proper breathing, 91
right amount, 140, 343
when hands feel numb, 51

humor and joy

benefits of, 57, 227
as teaching tool, 198
cheerful heart, a tonic, 351
children, a humor source, 116
delight in children, 376
importance of joy, 175
laugh a day, 80
laughter, best tonic, 405
lessening children's gloom, 383
need for laughing parents, 277
witticisms
about housework, 30
about conversing with doctor, 345

medical tips

appendicitis 224

Special tips for Parenting Children Through Grades 1–6

Special Tips for Parenting Teenagers

Pearls of Wisdom

Random reflections